I WANT TO KNOW

Are Ghosts Real?

Heather Moore Niver

Enslow Publishing
101 W. 23rd Street
Suite 240
New York, NY 10011
USA
enslow.com

Published in 2017 by Enslow Publishing, LLC
101 W 23rd St. Suite 240 New York, NY 10011

Library of Congress Cataloging-in-Publication Data

Names: Niver, Heather Moore, author.
Title: Are ghosts real? / Heather Moore Niver.
Description: New York : Enlsow Publishing, 2017. | Series: I want to know | Includes
bibliographical references and index.
Identifiers: LCCN 2016024748 | ISBN 9780766082380 (library bound) | ISBN
9780766082366 (pbk.) | ISBN 9780766082373 (6-pack)
Subjects: LCSH: Ghosts—Juvenile literature.
Classification: LCC BF1461 .N58 2016 | DDC 133.1—dc23
LC record available at https://lccn.loc.gov/2016024748

Printed in China

To Our Readers: We have done our best to make sure all websites in this book were
active and appropriate when we went to press. However, the author and the publisher
have no control over and assume no liability for the material available on those websites or on any websites they may link to. Any comments or suggestions can be sent by
e-mail to customerservice@enslow.com.

Photo Credits: Cover, p. 4 Tom Tom/Shutterstock.com; pp. 3, 7 Hulton Archive/Getty
Images; p. 8 Jan Sochor/Latincontent/Getty Images; p. 9 gmnicholas/E+/Getty Images; p. 12 vitalez/Shutterstock.com; p. 13 Bettmannn/Getty Images; p. 15 jan kranen-
donk/Shutterstock.com; p. 16 Karen Grigoryan/Shutterstock.com; p. 17 Morgan Moss;
p. 19 Image Source/Getty Images; p. 20 Peter Baker/Getty Images; p. 21 andreiuc88/
Shutterstock.com; p. 22 Lario Tus/Shutterstock.com; p. 23 Everett Historical/Shutter-
stock.com; p. 25 Paolo Gallo/Shutterstock.com; p. 26 Gwoeii/Shutterstock.com; p. 29
Bajrich/Shutterstock.com.

Contents

Chapter 1

What Is a Ghost?

Have you ever seen, felt, or heard something that you just could not explain? A strange noise in the night? The shadow of a figure out of the corner of your eye? Sudden, unexplained coldness? Some people think these occurrences do have an explanation: ghosts.

Ghosts are in many stories, books, television shows, and movies. Some are sinister, while other **spirits** are considered good. Some people do not believe in ghosts. But of all **paranormal** occurrences, more people believe in ghosts than any other. In a 2005 survey, 32 percent of people questioned said that they believed in ghosts, about 48 percent said they did not, and 19 percent were not sure. What about you? Do you believe, or do you think those strange occurances are just coincidence?

Getting to Know Ghosts

Many people believe in ghosts, but what are they? *Merriam-Webster's Dictionary* defines a ghost as "a **disembodied** soul; especially: the **soul** of a dead person believed to be an inhabitant of the unseen world or to appear to the living in bodily likeness." A ghost is said to live in the **netherworld**, but it can visit the living, too.

Some ghosts are said to haunt places where they had a connection when they were alive. Ghosts might appear to look like they did in life. Or they might show up as **poltergeists**, which make noises, move around a building, or break things.

Imagine That!

The word "ghost" has been in use since the late sixteenth century. It comes from the ancient word *gast*, which means "guest" in the language that evolved into German.

Strange Stories

The idea that sometimes spirits survive death and live without a physical body resulted in ghost stories. These chilling tales have been around almost as long as there were stories to tell. Ancient people told stories of spirits and hauntings. They appear in the Bible, William Shakespeare's play *Hamlet*, and Charles Dickens's *A Christmas Carol*. Ghosts are found in stories all over the world. It seems that ghosts and their stories have been scaring people since the beginning of time.

The opening scene from William Shakespeare's famous play *Hamlet* begins with the appearance of the ghost of the recently dead king.

Possessed Person

When somebody is considered "possessed," it means the person is controlled by an evil spirit or even a demon. Sometimes possession is given as a reason for weird or otherwise unusual behavior. This can include strange speech or groaning. In some cultures, possession occurs because the person committed a type of religious crime.

Sometimes people report seeing orbs. Orbs are circles of light that cannot be explained. These mysterious circles often show up in photographs or on the sides of houses. Other people say they have experienced a ghost when they feel a cold spot in an otherwise warm room.

In Arabic folklore ghouls, or *ghūls*, haunt many stories. They are believed to live in deserted places, like burial grounds. Ghouls were considered evil spirits that could change the way they

It is common to hear about glowing balls of light, especially in cemeteries. Believers think that these orbs are the spirits of the dead.

appeared to the living. In other cultures, ghouls may not have any form at all.

In Germany, the kobold actually helps with chores around the house and sings to children. This playful spirit also hides tools or knocks things over. If the kobold is not fed, though, it becomes angry.

In Irish tradition, a ghost called a banshee predicts the deaths of members of certain families. The people of Papua New Guinea fear spirits of the jungle, called *dama dagenda*, who attack any trespassers who enter their land. In China, any person who accidentally dies spends three years after his or her death on the fringes of the underworld.

The poltergeist is a spirit that usually sticks to making noises, movements, or breaking items in a way that the living cannot explain. Typically, it only pesters one person in the family. Poltergeists are usually harmless.

Chapter 2

· · · · · · · · · · ·

Haunted Places

Any place where ghosts are said to appear is referred to as haunted. Ghosts or other mysterious **auras** have been recorded in buildings of all sizes.

A haunted house is connected with a ghost or other haunting spirit that was associated with it in life. The connection can be positive, but often it is negative. Sometimes the ghost haunts a place because it associates strong emotions with it, such as guilt, fear, sadness, or intense shock after dying in a horrible way. A ghost may haunt a place or the people there if it thinks they are in some way responsible for its tragic life or death.

Ghosts might appear as a dim **apparition** or a dark shadow. They might move things around. They might scream, laugh, or even make music.

Historic Haunts

One of the most famous haunted houses in the world is in Amityville, New York. On

November 14, 1974, a family of six was murdered in their home. The murderer was twenty-three-year-old Butch DeFeo, eldest son of the family. The house was sold the next year to George and Kathy Lutz. They soon moved in with their four children, but they experienced some horrors of their own. They claimed that cabinet doors slammed, and one door came off its hinges. Gooey green

112 Ocean Avenue, Amityville, New York, is one of the most famous "haunted" houses in the world, having inspired several books and films.

slime dripped from the ceilings. They said they saw demonic faces and swarms of insects that attacked them.

In the end, the truth was that the Lutz family, Butch DeFeo, and his lawyer all made up the story. The family made a lot of money from the story. The terrifying tall tale was made into many books and movies.

Centuries of Scares

It's no huge surprise that a nine-hundred-year-old castle in Scotland has its share of spirits. The most haunted house in Scotland was built in the twelfth century. Edinburgh Castle has survived all kinds of attacks, wars, and political changes over the centuries.

In 2001, a team of researchers searched secret passages and forgotten areas of the castle. They recorded the experiences of visitors, who were not told where the researchers recorded paranormal activity. Just over half of the witnesses said they experienced events in the areas that were considered haunted by researchers. More than a third reported hauntings in areas where

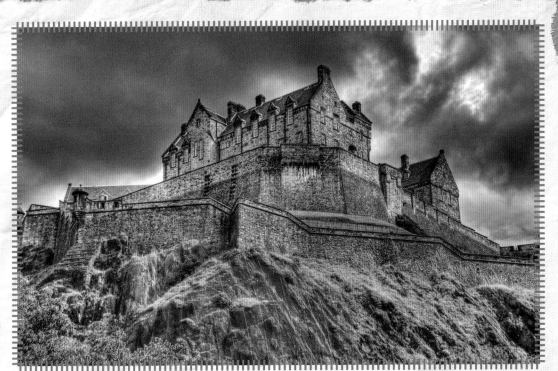

Many guests at Edinburgh Castle report paranormal experiences like drastic changes in temperature, appartitions and shadows, and ghostly fingers touching them.

researchers did not record activity. Visitors to the castle often report feeling cold spots and tugging on their clothes. They see ghostly figures.

Meanwhile, in London, England, the Tower of London has been home to ghosts for centuries. The ghosts of famous historical figures have been seen.

One part of the Tower of London is rumored to be haunted by a bear! A guard may have died from the shock of seeing the bear's ghost.

In Paris, France, six million people are buried along 180 miles (290 kilometers) of dark, winding tunnels, called catacombs. Bones line the deep and terrifying tunnels of the Paris Catacombs. Visitors have said they felt like hands they could not see were touching them. Others have sensed they were being followed. A few unfortunate visitors have felt like they were being strangled!

White House Hauntings

America's most famous house, the White House in Washington, DC, also has its haunts. John Adams's wife, Abigail, is reported to do laundry there. Dolley Madison's sprit is said to haunt the Rose Garden. And of course, Abe Lincoln's ghost might visit the Lincoln Bedroom.

Murders at Myrtles

In St. Louisville, Louisiana, the Myrtles Plantation is rumored to have had been the site of ten murders! So, of course, it has its share of ghost stories. The most famous ghost at Myrtles is Chloe. She was a slave whose master may have hacked off her ear. This was her punishment after she was caught **eavesdropping**. The angry Chloe

Said to be one of America's most haunted homes, Myrtles Plantation is rumored to have been built on a Tunica Indian burial ground. Can you spot the ghost in this picture?

may have poisoned a cake, which killed two of her master's daughters. As the story goes, the other slaves hanged her. Chloe's ghost is reported to haunt the farm. She wears a hat to hide her missing ear.

The story all started with a photograph taken in 1992. The photo shows the figure of a slave standing between two buildings. A film crew from *National Geographic Explorer* confirmed that there is a ghost girl in the photo.

Interested in more horrifying historic haunts? Look up Eastern State Penitentiary, Gettysburg Battlefield, Old Changi Hospital, the Queen Mary, the Whaley House, and the Winchester House.

Chapter 3

Ghost Hunters and Paranormal Investigators

Ghost hunting is something almost anyone can do. Expert ghost hunters warn that you should never go ghost hunting on your own. They suggest going out with people who have a lot of ghost-hunting experience at first. And even after that, always go with a partner. Anytime is a fine time for ghost hunting. The best hours, however, are between 9 p.m. and 6 a.m. These are called the "psychic hours." Photos taken of ghosts usually come out better in the dark.

Tools of the Trade

Some ghost hunters use simple equipment like cameras, voice recorders, and flashlights. Others get far more technical. They use instruments called Geiger counters, electromagnetic field (EMF) detectors, ion detectors, and super-sensitive microphones. The EMF meter might be the most popular ghost-hunting tool.

Imagine That!

Some ghost hunters put a special colored lens, often green, over their flashlight. This helps them see without the bright light ruining their sight in the dark.

Hunting Haunts

First, check out the haunted area during the day. Watch for dangerous areas or anything that might trip you up in the dark. Always be sure that you are not going in a place where you aren't allowed. Ghost hunters should get permission from the landowners to hunt there.

Everyone participating in the ghost hunt should agree on a time and place to meet. Many ghost hunters say a prayer when they enter a location. This can be said privately or as a group. Some ghost hunters believe that a prayer can keep them safe from evil spirits.

Spend some time walking around the area to get to know the space. You can take notes during this time and set up equipment like cameras. Then get to work! Write down anything that seems unusual. Suggestions include different temperatures as well as whatever you see or hear. Note if you have any strange feelings or emotions. In general, note anything that seems weird or out of the ordinary.

A timeline notes the exact times that incidents happened. Even make a note of a cough! When you compare notes with your partners, you will know if the cough was from one of you or from a ghost.

When you are done, meet up with everyone. Some experts suggest that before you leave, ask the spirits not to follow you home.

Ghosts on the Go

Of course there are phone apps for ghost hunting! Some let you record sounds. Others let you ask ghosts questions. Some provide information about the ghosts around you, like when they lived, or how they died.

Chapter 4

Explaining the Unexplainable

Plenty of people believe they have seen ghosts. When former British prime minister Winston Churchill was visiting the White House, he stepped out of the bathtub and saw the ghost of President Abraham Lincoln! He kept his wits about him. He said, "Good evening, Mr. President. You seem to have me at a disadvantage." After that, he said the ghost simply smiled and disappeared.

Scientists have studied some reasons why people believe in ghosts. Tiredness, drugs, alcohol, or poor lighting can sometimes be a simple explanation for what people claim to see.

The Nitty Gritty of Ghosts

Other people claim to have had repeated experiences seeing ghosts. Ghost **skeptics** have some logical explanations for that, too. Seeing objects move might be linked to the brain. When some parts of the brain are damaged, the person can have vision troubles. These might be mistaken for ghosts. One kind of brain disorder, called **epilepsy**, might give people a creepy feeling that there is someone nearby or that shadowy people are with them.

What about evidence from photographs? Sometimes the photographer changes the photograph to make it look like there is an apparition. Photo-editing programs on computers make this easy.

Imagine That!

One problem with proving whether ghosts exist is that they move. One person might think he sees a ghost. But when another person is in the same spot, the ghost may have moved.

One method for making an image look like there is a ghost is called **double exposure**. In a double exposure, an image is repeated by exposing it to light more than once. This makes it look as though there is a ghost in the photograph.

Orbs are bright, white, round lights. They can be created by dust on or very close to a camera lens. It's easy to create your own orb by using a flash when taking a photo on a rainy night.

Moldy and Old

In some old houses, there may be a scientific explanation for ghosts right under your nose. Researchers have studied the air

Photo Proof?

In 1947 a mother took a picture of the gravestone of one of her children. When she got the photo developed, she saw a child she didn't recognize standing near the grave! It wasn't one of her children. Also, the mother had never taken a photograph of her children.

Did the hairs on the back of your neck stand up? Did you hear a faint moan? Did you see a shadow move out of the corner of your eye? It could be a ghost!

in old houses. They found that some types of mold are poisonous when you breathe them in. These molds can affect the brain. They make people believe they are seeing things that are not there—like ghosts! Breathing in mold can also cause problems with moving, confusion, and balance. Some of these effects might explain the "creepy" feeling some people associate with ghosts. Maybe there are similar molds in houses reported to be haunted. If you feel these feelings often, be sure and tell a parent or adult and see a doctor.

Proof of the Paranormal

Skeptics point out that ghost hunters find a lot of evidence of ghosts. But they do not seem to come away from hunts with much proof. Skeptics think some of the evidence is a trick of a person's mind. But people still have experiences and share their stories, all over the world. There isn't any proof that ghosts exist. But there isn't really proof they don't, either. What do you believe?

Words to Know

apparition A surprising or unusual sight, such as a ghost of someone who has died.

aura A bright light or energy.

disembodied Without a physical, or human, life.

double exposure An image that is repeated by exposing it to light more than once. This makes it look as though there is a ghost in the photograph.

eavesdrop To listen in on someone else's conversation.

epilepsy A brain disorder.

netherworld A world where only the dead live.

paranormal Event that cannot be explained by science.

poltergeist A playful ghost that makes noises or throws things around.

skeptic Someone who does not easily believe in something.

soul A person's spirit.

spirit A part of a human's soul that lives on after death.

Further Reading

Books:

Dooling, Sandra. *Haunted Houses!* New York, NY: Powerkids Press, 2014.

Fontes, Justine. *Casebook: Ghosts and Poltergeists.* New York, NY: Windmill Books, 2010.

Ganeri, Anita. *Ghosts and Other Specters.* New York, NY: Powerkids Press, 2011.

Perritano, John. *Amityville.* New York, NY: Powerkids Press, 2015.

Websites:

Haunted History

alaskahistoricalsociety.org/discover-alaska/kids-page/haunted-history/

Read about hauntings in the state of Alaska!

The Science of Ghosts and Hauntings

www.unmuseum.org/ghosts.htm

Learn more about ghosts, haunted houses, and the science behind ghosts.

Scientific Proof for Ghosts?

channel.nationalgeographic.com/videos/scientific-proof-for-ghosts/

Follow National Geographic and some scientists as they search for proof that ghosts exist.

Index